Mammals

by Kari Schuetz

BELLWETHER MEDIA • MINNEAPOLIS, MN

Note to Librarians, Teachers, and Parents:

Blastoff! Readers are carefully developed by literacy experts and combine standards-based content with developmentally appropriate text.

Level 1 provides the most support through repetition of high-frequency words, light text, predictable sentence patterns, and strong visual support.

Level 2 offers early readers a bit more challenge through varied simple sentences, increased text load, and less repetition of high-frequency words.

Level 3 advances early-fluent readers toward fluency through increased text and concept load, less reliance on visuals, longer sentences, and more literary language.

Level 4 builds reading stamina by providing more text per page, increased use of punctuation, greater variation in sentence patterns, and increasingly challenging vocabulary.

Level 5 encourages children to move from "learning to read" to "reading to learn" by providing even more text, varied writing styles, and less familiar topics.

Whichever book is right for your reader, Blastoff! Readers are the perfect books to build confidence and encourage a love of reading that will last a lifetime!

This edition first published in 2013 by Bellwether Media, Inc.

No part of this publication may be reproduced in whole or in part without written permission of the publisher. For information regarding permission, write to Bellwether Media, Inc., Attention: Permissions Department, 5357 Penn Avenue South, Minneapolis, MN 55419.

Library of Congress Cataloging-in-Publication Data
Schuetz, Kari.
  Mammals / by Kari Schuetz.
     p. cm. – (Blastoff! readers: animal classes)
  Includes bibliographical references and index.
  Summary: "Simple text and full-color photography introduce beginning readers to mammals. Developed by literacy experts for students in kindergarten through third grade"–Provided by publisher.
  ISBN 978-1-60014-775-3 (hardcover : alk. paper)
  1. Mammals–Juvenile literature. I. Title.
  QL706.2S336 2013
  599–dc23
                                              2011053040

Printed in the United States of America, North Mankato, MN.

Table of Contents

The Animal Kingdom

Every living and **extinct** animal belongs to the animal kingdom.

Members of the animal kingdom
are grouped by how they are alike.

What Are Mammals?

Mammals make up one major **class** in the animal kingdom. They and other animals with backbones are **vertebrates**.

The Animal Kingdom

vertebrates

examples of animals with backbones

amphibians

birds

fish

mammals

reptiles

invertebrates

examples of animals without backbones

arachnids

crustaceans

insects

Mammals are **warm-blooded** animals. They keep a constant body temperature.

All mammals have hair or fur on their bodies. Even **aquatic** mammals have hair.

Mammals have lungs to breathe air. Those that live underwater must come to the surface to breathe.

Female mammals have **mammary glands**. Mothers nurse their young with milk from these organs.

Groups of Mammals

platypus

Mammals are organized into three groups based on how they begin life.

Platypuses and spiny anteaters are **monotremes**. These animals hatch from eggs that their mothers lay.

spiny anteater

Marsupials are born before they fully develop. Most live inside a **pouch** on their mother's belly after they are born.

kangaroo

pouch

koalas

Kangaroos, koalas, and opossums are all marsupials.

15

Most mammals are **placentals**. They develop inside their mother's **womb**. The **placenta** gives them **nutrients**. Their mothers give birth to them once they are fully developed.

The largest animal in the world is a mammal. It can weigh up to 400,000 pounds (181,437 kilograms) and has a heart the size of a small car. It is the blue whale!

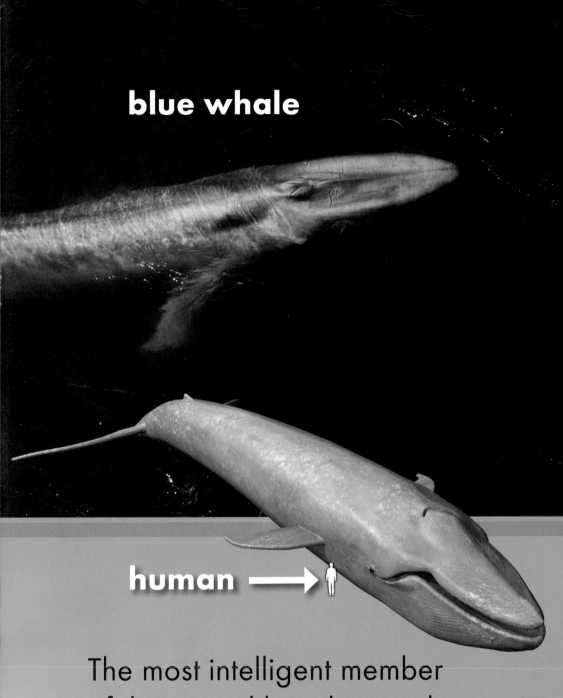

blue whale

human ⟶

The most intelligent member of the animal kingdom is also a mammal. It is the human. Yes, you are a mammal!

Marvelous Mammals

Smallest:
bumblebee bat

Largest on Land:
African elephant

Tallest:
giraffe

Hairiest:
sea otter

Fastest:
cheetah

Slowest:
three-toed sloth

**three-toed
sloth**

African elephant

Glossary

aquatic—living in water

class—a group within the animal kingdom; members of a specific class share many of the same characteristics.

extinct—no longer existing on Earth

mammary glands—organs that female mammals have to produce milk

marsupials—mammals that are born before they have fully developed in the womb; most marsupials finish developing inside their mother's belly pouch.

monotremes—mammals that hatch from eggs that their mothers lay

nutrients—elements that plants and animals need to live and grow

placenta—the organ through which placentals are fed in their mother's womb

placentals—mammals that are born once they have fully developed inside their mother's womb

pouch—a pocket on the belly of a female marsupial; a newborn marsupial spends the beginning of its life in its mother's pouch.

vertebrates—members of the animal kingdom that have backbones

warm-blooded—able to maintain a constant body temperature in both warm and cold climates

womb—the organ inside a female where a baby grows

To Learn More

AT THE LIBRARY
Carwardine, Mark. *Animal Records.* New York, N.Y.:
Sterling, 2008.

McGhee, Karen, and George McKay. *Encyclopedia
of Animals.* Washington, D.C.: National Geographic,
2007.

Taylor, Barbara. *The Mammal Book: Jaws, Paws,
Claws and More...* London, U.K.: Carlton Books,
2010.

ON THE WEB
Learning more about mammals
is as easy as 1, 2, 3.

1. Go to www.factsurfer.com.

2. Enter "mammals" into the search box.

3. Click the "Surf" button and you will
   see a list of related Web sites.

With factsurfer.com, finding more
information is just a click away.

Index